Birds Knit My Ribs Together

Phil Barnett

ARACHNE PRESS

First published in UK 2024 by Arachne Press Limited
100 Grierson Road, London, SE23 1NX
www.arachnepress.com

ISBNs
Print: 978-1-913665-91-3 eBook: 978-1-913665-92-0

Printed on woodfree paper in the UK

Thanks to Muireann Grealy for her proofreading.

With thanks to
Alan, Cherry, Jackie and Mark

Birds Knit My Ribs Together

Contents

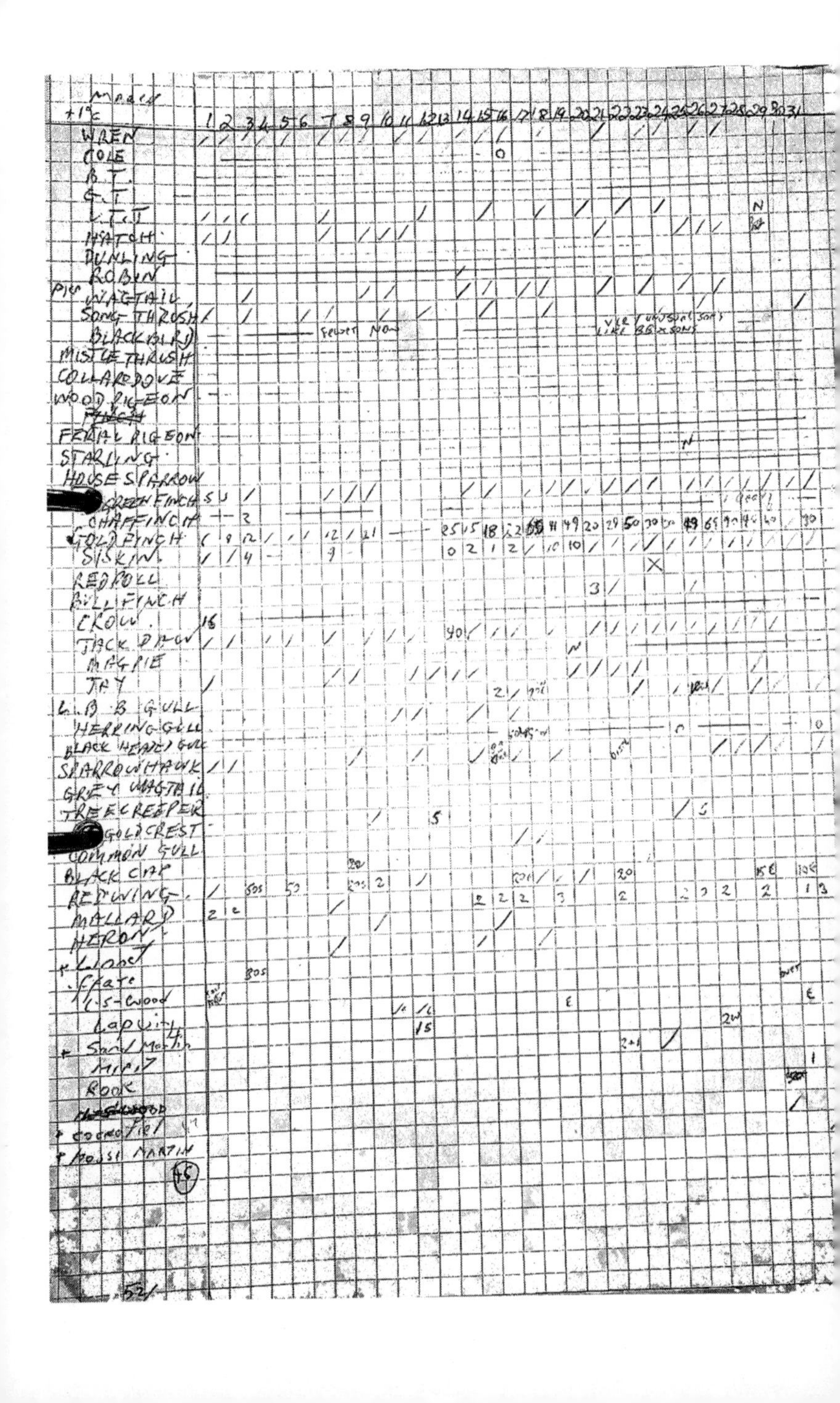

March
+1%

1 2 3 4 5 6 7 8 9 10 11 12 13 14 15 16 17 18 19 20 21 22 23 24 25 26 27 28 29 30 31

WREN
COLE
B.T.
G.T.
L.T.T
NATCH
DUNLING
ROBIN
PIE WAGTAIL
SONG THRUSH
BLACKBIRD
MISTLE THRUSH
COLLARD DOVE
WOOD PIGEON
~~FINCH~~
FERAL PIGEON
STARLING
HOUSE SPARROW
GREENFINCH
CHAFFINCH
GOLDFINCH
SISKIN
REDPOLL
BULLFINCH
CROW
JACK DAW
MAGPIE
JAY
L.B.B. GULL
HERRING GULL
BLACK HEADED GULL
SPARROW HAWK
GREY WAGTAIL
TREECREEPER
GOLDCREST
COMMON GULL
BLACK CAP
REDWING
MALLARD
HERON
+ Linnet
Grate
L.S. Wood
Lapwing
+ Sand Martin
Mipit
Rook
~~[illegible]~~
+ Cuckoo
+ House Martin
45

SEVERE NOW

VERY UNUSUAL SONGS LIKE BB & SONGS

52

Introduction

Wren, Coal Tit, Blue Tit, Goldcrest
At the start of each month I say the names of birds.
Great Tit, Long Tailed Tit, Nuthatch, Tree Creeper
My mother writes them down
Blackbird, Song Thrush, Mistle Thrush, Blackcap
For me to tick each day I see the bird.
Robin, Dunnock, Pied Wagtail, House Sparrow
I can't write them myself, my brain won't work.
Greenfinch, Chaffinch, Goldfinch, Bullfinch
I can't move, I watch birds.
Wood Pigeon, Collared Dove, Feral Pigeon, Sparrow Hawk
At the start of each month I recite the scope of my world,
the extent of my landmass, my ancient map.
Lesser Black Backed Gull, Herring Gull, Black Headed Gull,
Heron
At the start of each month I say the names of birds.
Jay, Magpie, Jackdaw, Crow.

The Pond

by the pond in always falling daylight
misted moon-smitten blue

all the animals came and went
and all the ghosts
glancing through curves
through bent branches of night-heavy alder
things that were neither

everything went to that watering place

there were false alarms, many of them
a flock of birds on the in breath
a lost decade on the out

dipping down to sip
the last end-of-summer swallow
just skimming the surface
of a stillborn dawn

then at last a song thrush sang
it's day, it's day
and because this time I sang along

it was day

Dream Thrush

back then there were only wild words

mostly wordless, free of meaning
grounded air, a ripple's seeing-through-to

an omen-thrush, a new dawn-thrush

winter's tale breast, yarn of flank
a story-thrush, an idea of feathers
more of them with each telling

till I was a full-thrush

a song-thrush now,
bird shape of the farthest branches

spoke them once, sang them twice
these words
I gave his grandson to sing

Wounds

blue-brittle sky banged with a hammer
knocks out a piece
falls to the ground
mouth open gulping

I found a god on the path
a small one
fluttering broken blooded
grounded pilot behind enemy lines
eyes like a drowned village

I picked it up, cupped
as if holding a fledgling angel
this lost jigsaw piece of sky
this little god of hurt
with scar tissue dreams
turning wounds into stories

it lifted a wing, pleading
I pulled out a thorn
jabbed it into my heart

Two White Horses

without tv or news or clocks
time is measured in white horses
in the field below
the morning brings a new alignment

they are enacting all the prepositions
in front of, behind, next to
and some that only horses know
the stations of the horse

two entangled particles play out
a stately ballet on the clock-face field
clouds attracted by a strong force
and repelled by a weak one

next day they put on adverbs of time
before, after, a long time ago
a very very long time ago

and on the last day
they're performing verbs
galloping, slowing, resting, lying down

leaving the house for the last time
I turn, to see a waft of white smoke
that turns into a tail, then two of them

twirling, tick-tocking the seconds
or is it the years

Curse

earth's core pulls me towards itself
the unwanted embrace,
gravity, I curse you
you've run me aground

I feel every dead-hand ounce
heavy hailstones inside me
weight is my enemy
each cell is a rock
and I have dropped anchor
probably for good

overhead house martins
play chase with here and over there
batting away distance for the fun of it
while I live encased in granite
I curse house martins

why can't I turn a dial, flick a switch, say a prayer
why can't I walk
and be well

life, I curse you too
you punctured me
the air that rushed out was all that I had
all that I was

nothing left but the deflated balloon
of what was once a life

To Know What it's Like

I threw myself to the wind
to see what it was like
scooped up autumn leaves
imagining they were ashes
arms flung wide, prising open the air
to take the offering
of a me I'd cremated
to know what it was like
threw them into the embrace of falling
threw them to a corner of empty
like a self's sky burial

felt
nothing
gave
up

watched a jackdaw tumbling
juggling gravity
playing cards with up and down
friendly with sky in all directions
making a balloon of itself
tapping the bottom into buoyancy
watched and knew what it was like

Box of Letting Go

I bought a box of letting go
from a pet shop in Greece
horizon-eyed goldfinch inside
scooped off a sky, stuffed into cardboard

took it to the town's edge
a suspicion of locals watched

opened the lid, then jack-in-a-box
that kept on going as cloudward rocket
hallelujahs in its wake,
bicycle bell expletives

me down there holding on
with a box I paid good money for
just to watch it let go

Jackdaws to Roost

tea leaf residues at the bottom
of the day's cup
after the light has been poured off
as flecks of night, as jackdaws,
their dusk flight to roost

yesterday, a tight flock,
a thunder cloud's worth
of omens

today, dawdling twos and threes
all down the sky's street
like homeward schoolchildren

always a fresh augury
there above the land turn's knuckle
in cloud sunken bird shapes,
air cast, dark-parsed runes

and tomorrow?
ask the sky

Bird Watching

my bone-bag by a window
skin, blood, organs where I left them
when I could walk

three panes of glass, one large, two small
a meagre insect's compound eye

diagonal flightpath of sparrow
plots a graph, charting my decline

out there in the garden
electrical impulses, shooting stars
neurons have wings

consciousness outsourced to birds
comets across the mind's dark sky

We Give What We Can

cross my palm with robin
just one pin, just one needle
tiny claw-prickle human hand

blood-orange-bib bird
across my heart line
along my love line

this pumpkin-sky morning
sunrise has trusted me
with a fragment of itself

we give what gifts we can
me, a crumb of cheese
the robin, one drop of life's spittle

a wild bird comes to my hand
and for a moment
I am wild too

Just Sitting

a prosecco world, still all winter
stirred in March, shaken in April
this morning the cork comes out
fizzing spring morning, jug after jug
poured through a bright hole in the sky

I want to share in it, to taste it
like spilt wine licked off the table
greedily before it's gone

but today I cannot walk
not through those cloister woods to
my bluebell church, music-deep in blackcap
that hoverfly and stitchwort springcraft
nor will I headlong into spears of it

here in this garden I'll let nature wait on me
hand and foot, and all the senses

the tincture of skylark, dripping song
neat, straight on to eardrums
listening for that part with the long notes
where for a moment the whole world warps
into one long note

I'm rooted to the spot, but I have roots
today I cannot walk
everything is here

Under Wings

a pepper grinder
somewhere to the north
a few turns
sky sprinkled with thrush
air seasoned with flickering wings

not yet enough
more turns
another jostling, journeying constellation
pipits, redwings, fieldfares
migrating flocks

brief intersection of grounded man
and flying bird
a fractional part-share
in a pair of wings

Trepanning

birds knit my ribs together
wrapped the corpse in feathers
embalming in song; mummifying

wrens sipped cuckoo spit
spat it to a thimble

stirred in berry and honeydew
dripped the tincture drip by drop

a woodpecker bored my skull
in trepanation

drummed a hole and wasps flew out

goldcrests' needle-calls put punctures
all along the kidney's line

swallow's flightlines skywrote my ill
when thrushes sang it out loud

a woodpigeon listened while
I told it secrets
laughed when I lied

Unchorused

what if
I actually – am – a bird
my cupped hands
opening to release me
as newly feathered friend of the sky
inventing geometry
arcing around the bottom of a cloud

what if
I've been calling to myself
all this time
to finally fledge, finally fly
the quiet one left behind in the
bosom-warm, womb-safe nest

if
I actually – am – a bird
then what happened to
those dawns unchorused
where did they go,
all those unsung songs?

A Crack Must Have Opened

a crack must have opened
to let the barn owl in
slipped
white side down
ghost side up
mothborne from another world
while
flashes like bonfire night
in very slow motion
unleaded the clouds
tiny nativities make
day-fragments glow
scattered at first then melding
to an alleluia of skylight
the owl made a vortex
of itself
spiral tightened down by the pull
of the volewise grass
then dipping back
changes shape
to air-snipping scissoring shears
maybe it passed on
a baton of morning
to the kestrel

Plugged by a Bird

downwater of wind
is a kingfisher shaped gap
plugged by a bird

a hole this world

would otherwise
drain through

just perching there
density of deep earth core
compressed, gravity on gravity
into rainbow's diamond

only a bird stands between us
and death

Unsprung

a dead heron has dropped out of a heron
in the hug of a stream's curve

prone sprawl of
unsprung neck, unwaded legs, unflighted wings

still point at the centre of a wheeling world
celebrant to movement's congregation
and pivot to animation's choir

damselflies darn the air
fixing rips with yarn of blue atmosphere

as stream-rippled reflected suns
all the constellations arise and pass away
in the meander at a heron's fulcrum

Butcherbird

he hangs his mind out to dry
sodden as a peat bog
so wet more wet won't make it wetter

hangs it on a branch
fixed twice with makeshift pegs
spliced bark peeled from sycamore
bound with dead dogwood cord

an owl's feathers
fly silent as a secret
leaving a mind-owl naked and flailing
a commotion
of skewered selfhood
"I, me, me, me!"

he had every intention
of going back
but he's now butcherbird
to himself

Terrible Curve

a terrible curve
white body extrudes brontosaurus neck
up and round to the head
head like an ice-breaker
ship glued to a standstill
a Pompeii figure
half an embracing couple
caught in the act of being alive
dead swan frozen in ice

through binoculars
a closed eye that would have watched
its own slow fossilisation

eye
opens

this quarter inch part of a whole
planet's worth of movement
is the only part that moves
and the dead swan sees me

eye
closes

and the dead swan sees through me

Nor

between lochan stops, in a Morris Maxi
my family northbound to Fort William
I looked out of the window,
not in a human way
but like a blackbird
looking for worms on the lawn
staccato jerks of the head
tilt
stop
gaze
stop
turn
stop
they'll see my thrush-like movements
and think I'm a bird
I thought
(this was an aspiration)

many years later
travelling to Scotland again
I look out, not in a human way
nor like a blackbird

Woodcock Rising

leaning into the gale
that sabres rain as a weapon
each up tilt of the head
met with wind-slap-spite

foliage resolves into bird
leaves revolve into woodcock
a long twig threads forward
in a form become beak

a maple red rump at the rear
is redder by far than it is

bracken stitched
tawny woven through fawn
and all the fallen leaves
that ever could be
on the back and wings

unplotted path jinked out
of bends and kinks as it
weaves through a barn dance
of willow arms

the woodcock clatters
quickly out of view
its second has scooped up the autumn
leaving a spring in the mind

Floating Cork of Me

standing still where low light
draws back all that's not dawn
to leave a clutch of autumn
in the nest of the world

a roe deer doe steps out,
like a bather caught unaware
sees me and dresses fast in
the robe of its caution

backwash step back in fear
incoming wave more curious
deer ebb, deer flow, inching to
look at the floating cork of me

me who only ever steps back

Molten Roe

soon as it sees me
the deer makes of itself
a ball of molten roe
hind, hide, head and hoof
are all in there now
pours itself into
an old mould it knows
has ample time to set
as time has also slowed
the new shape has the jump
of a curve
takes the springs from
a bound and bends them
to an arch
in mid air though
with a different gravity
that pushes not pulls
the leapingness spreads
not just the deer now
but all around
a rump ups
lift of back behind
white now coming through
it wasn't there before
but time has also stopped

So Close

dragonfly peels back the moment
arrives and claims the air

clatters right up to my face
staring-contest eyes
kestrel-steady, straight at me
so close I feel the wind of its
judgement

like that one when I was five or six
pulling scab off the past

what would it say
this drone
that reports back to time

You are not done
you still have many winds
to lean into to

Amber Under

amber under
burnt umber over
alder scribbled water

half moon high tide
washes up a morning,
message-in-a-bottle heron

follow the day
back to its source, drop of blood
on goldcrest crown

upstream of me
nothing to find
nothing to lose

The News

the news broke around six o'clock
robins heard it first
plucked colours from their breasts
then sang them to the dark

that coloured the tiny parts exposed
by dawn's needle
etching
clouds whispered the light
held on to it for a while
then passed it on
leaking ochre rumours
bleeding into flame
the hills heard the word
lifted the veil
but slowly
a star burst the horizon
flooded a length of it
fireworked the fields
crackerjacked through trees
fire-flyed the mist
even glow-wormed webs
the news broke around six o'clock
everyone knew by seven

Spans Two Hills

the way that
moon sets at sunrise
night and day, children on a seesaw
and citrus-zested sky is
blood-orange banded, rind speckled
over first-misted dawncast

the way that
a cloud shadow
spans two hills, rains on one
and a curlew calls
in the cleft's stream-rinsed tilt

the way that
the flushed snipe pinballs
off an invisible stairwell
that slants as it climbs up
silent zig, sound on the zag

the way that
lingering mist is
called to come home
by the just-risen sun
like a child that played out too long
and just before it floats up it tilts

Its Own Angle

chips off the block of jackdaw-rock
flung over a sandstone sky
each with its own angle
then mackerel-shoal switch
and the whole flock is an angle

   not like that

digits of woodland below
where oaks and beeches
queue round the contours
four bars of birdsong
finished with a drum-fill
in woodpecker time

   not like that

brown and speckled oval
shoots up from bramble
a leap
the first part is salmon
a flap
the second is thrush

   it's happened before
   but not like that

The Nature Dog

wind licks my face
the only part exposed under woollen hat
and above my layers of rebuttal

like a dog
that wants to taste animal
not man-made fibre
wants to mix salts with something alive

a lower case letter of geese written
one woodcock above the bend of horizon
calls voicing a grey sky's falling
smash through mind's brittle glass
to speak with the bones and
know the blood-brothers

  nature is saying hello

I'm brought hard to a halt in
a tangle of bramble attrition
a Gulliver needled, pinned down
by a shoal's tooth thorn-pricks
that scratch-card off my complacency
my human skins

  nature is saying hello

the nature dog
bright eyed, glad to see us
always jumping up to greet us
forgiving every rebuff

always seeking out the
exposed part
  to say hello

Coastal Footpath

all these plucked lives,
these men, women, children
now held up like flowers

on the coastal footpath
as they go past the window,
fleshed out shadows

all
with an angle to the ground,
accounting for conditions
correcting for the slope

lone man with rucksack
filled up with his mind,
a stoop of person

flight of geese, in and out of formation
calling each other home,
that family of four

still green into windblown green,
chord progressions though grass,
the gap between that couple

they go by
always
correcting for the slope

Used To Be

above farm-forgotten fields
where the earth curves
a winged upbeat finds the crow
a downbeat finds the wind

sky's very bottom fringed
with a childhood of butterflies
and buttercup tops that polka round
each other in more than double time

grasshopping chirps and bumble of bees,
with hoverfly-hum – all in a hymn;
hymn enough to make remembered air
uncase the amber of long ago

Flux

trees jigsaw the sky, gatekeeping the sun,
cast a mosaic of brief magpies onto the path
bright bubbles up on dark
like fragments of day engulfing a night
then total eclipses and fast crescent moons

I close my eyes

breath ebbs, on the shore inside,
waves backwash along the shingle-mind
moments form like eggs and then hatch,
cuckoo-kicked out by the next in the clutch

all that's still is moving, portions are fusing
spilling out to a fountain of flux

I open my eyes

Set the Air

morning mist lifts leaving remnants as dew
sleep around the corners of awakening

small clouds are snared in thistle-cleft
and hogweed-crook, connected by beelines

grass is half grass – half silk
a house being painted, white sheets
draped over furniture

a transformation has set the air
so now the world is bound round in web

I came this way yesterday
but through different fields
not spider-worked like these

they were there, yes
but not on the planet we know
with people, dogs, roads and bottles

now on this fizzing morning there's a glass
to be raised to the part of the iceberg
that isn't the tip

to all the slept-through moths and bats
everything too small, too hidden
too much

Stones

I turn over stones looking for words
for the oyster, the one with pearl
in woodlouse-scurry and wormcast-coil
divining-rod to underbelly

a flock of falling leaves
the cold-day breath on autumn's last sigh
hoping one settles on my sleeve
one I can read before it snowflakes

I'm sure they are there, the words
but like the coat tails of a dream
waking's first few seconds separate
those fingertips of farewell

but
they are not there
not under stones
they are the stones,
they are the turning

I turn over stones

Open

a trickle of moments
seeps in at the first crack
in lockstep with a wren's song

open the window
let in the dam-burst dawn
you surface into
a spring morning at flood

there!

that shift, the lift
the world turns on a key change

A Willow's Word

I felt it first in autumn
beneath the willow's
stone-dead reach
on every twig of every branch
buds, tiny resurrections

but didn't breathe a word

then in winter's first bright dawn
lit through boughs
dewshot radials made a fan
to waft away the unlight

some whispers

When I was Water

broke my skull on stone
headfirst when I was water
splashed over soft-rime glaze
to the rigid standstill of frozen-fall

conditions I'd never before seen
not this cold

but I knew what to do –
when not to flow, but sculpt
hard flesh on three dimension's bones
ice roundels all around the seeded centre
as if molecules all had a handbrake
and to cohere the drops
I brought them to a stop
I seemed to know what water did
under these circumstances

using what I'd learnt
in the cleft of a flash-jagged fork
when I was lightning

Facts

this morning
a barn owl flew the moon home
and a wood pigeon clapped twice
to hey-presto the sun
landscape's liquid bubbled up
and set
as silhouetted deer

this morning
no facts checked out
everything was true

Wildlife

a bird fails to row through concrete
wings that have no more use for air
slap the path – a wrestler's signal to submit,
an upside down collared dove

panicked into glass
a stunned rebound,
ghost of the near-future,
fossil of that last successful wingbeat

intercepted by a sparrow hawk
and a two-bird scrimmage
dove a halo of feathers
as the hawk plucks

it is still alive

Birds

when the god drew the world in pencil
and coloured outside the lines
all the birds were born

as sparks up and down earth's nerves
electric signals to let land know
what sky is thinking

as stitches at the seam of night and day
darning blue rips
where comets tore through

and a balm of high-cloud breath
first flycatcher gathered
to soothe a sore world's gashes

all along the branch
curving round a planet
the event-horizon of flight

I Shall Know Less

this year I shall know fewer things
If I see a wren, I won't know it's a wren
or even whether it's a bird or
a swollen river's smooth-humped water
a baby's kick from inside a womb

If I walk by the canal
I won't know which are trees
and which reflection
or even if they're earth-steps of
ground trotting over my soles
with two bullfinches calling,
on either side

I'll forget which memories are mine
and which belong to the moon
was that me who got lost on Bodmin Moor
and prayed to a god
after praying her into being

or was it the shadow of a crow
merging with a cloud's dark edge

About Arachne Press

Arachne Press is a micro publisher of (award-winning!) short story and poetry anthologies and collections, novels including a Carnegie Medal nominated young adult novel, and a photographic portrait collection.

We are expanding our range all the time, but the short form is our first love. We keep fiction and poetry live, through readings, festivals (in particular our Solstice Shorts Festival), workshops, exhibitions and all things to do with writing.

https://arachnepress.com/

Follow us on Twitter:
@ArachnePress
@SolShorts

and Instagram
@ArachnePress

Like us on Facebook:
@ArachnePress
@SolsticeShorts2014